WORLD OF BELIEFS

In the same series:
- ○ Buddhism
- ○ Christianity
- ○ Islam

Published by Grange Books
an imprint of Grange Books Plc
The Grange
Kingsnorth Industrial Estate
Hoo, nr Rochester
Kent ME3 9ND
www.Grangebooks.co.uk

ISBN 1-84013-599-9
Grange Books edition printed in 2004

Copyright © 2001 by McRae Books Srl, Florence (Italy)

Judaism
was created and produced by McRae Books
Borgo Santa Croce, 8 – Florence (Italy)
info@mcraebooks.com

SERIES EDITOR Anne McRae
TEXT Cath Senker
ILLUSTRATIONS Studio Stalio (Alessandro Cantucci, Fabiano Fabbrucci, Andrea Morandi), Paola Ravaglia, Gian Paolo Faleschini
GRAPHIC DESIGN Marco Nardi
LAYOUT Laura Ottina, Adriano Nardi
REPRO Litocolor, Florence
PICTURE RESEARCH Loredana Agosta
Printed and bound in China

WORLD OF BELIEFS

Cath Senker

JUDAISM

Grange
BOOKS

TABLE OF CONTENTS

Note – This book shows dates as related to the conventional beginning of our era, or the year 0, understood as the year of Christ's birth. All events dating before this year are listed as BCE, or Before Current Era (ex. 928 BCE). Events dating after the year 0 are defined as CE, or Current Era (ex. 24 CE), wherever confusion might arise.

What is Judaism?

Judaism is the oldest monotheistic faith – the first with believers who worshiped one God alone. However, Judaism is not simply a religion. A Jewish person is someone with a Jewish mother. Judaism stresses descent rather than religion; **Jews** are born rather than made. The story of Judaism is the story of the Jewish people. This book examines the history of the Jewish people and their culture, religion, and traditions.

*An **Orthodox** Jew reading from the Torah, which is part of the Hebrew Bible. Orthodox Jews believe the Torah is the word of God as revealed to Moses on Mount Sinai. Part of this revered work is read each week in **synagogue**.*

Menorah

The **menorah** is a seven-branched candlestick, an ancient symbol of Judaism deriving from the menorah that originally stood in the **Temple in Jerusalem**. The menorah framed by two olive branches is the emblem of the state of **Israel**.

*Below: Orthodox Jews praying at the **Wailing Wall**. The Wailing Wall in Jerusalem is the most holy site for Jews. This wall is all that remains of the Second Temple, which was destroyed by the Romans in 70 CE.*

The Star of David became a symbol of Judaism during the Middle Ages. It signifies the protection of God given to David, King of Israel, c. 970 BCE. Many Jewish people wear the symbol to show they are proud to be Jewish, and it appears on the Israeli flag.

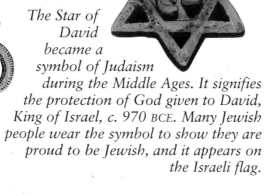

Left: The Tablets of the Law, engraved with the Ten Commandments. The Ten Commandments must be followed by every Jew, man or woman, young or old, at all times. Each Commandment is regarded as a subject heading, covering different aspects of the principle. For example, the command to keep the Sabbath suggests the idea of a holy day; this idea extends to all the festival days in Judaism.

Synagogues

Synagogues were developed after the First Temple was destroyed and the Jews were taken into captivity in Babylon. The synagogue is the place where Jewish people come together to study and worship. Devout Jews attend on Saturday, their holy day. Others attend only on important holy days and festivals. The synagogue is a community center – the home of Jews all over the world.

This photo shows the synagogue in Florence, Italy, on Saturday.

The mezuzah

There is a **mezuzah** on almost every doorpost in many Jewish homes. The mezuzah is a parchment scroll with the first two paragraphs of the Shema handwritten on it, declaring the oneness of God and the special relationship between God and the Jewish people. It is kept inside a protective case, which is what you see from the outside.

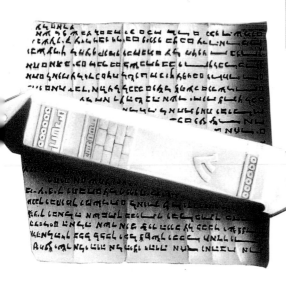

*Above: A mezuzah, shown with its case on top. The mezuzah is a holy object and the writing must remain readable. Every three years, Jews take down each mezuzah so that a **rabbi** or scribe can check them and write over any faded parts. If the ink has faded or cracked too much, a mezuzah will be replaced.*

The History of Hebrew

Hebrew was spoken and written in ancient **Palestine** for more than a thousand years. By about 500 BCE it had largely been replaced by Aramaic as a spoken language, but it remained the religious language of the Jews. Hebrew was revived as a spoken language in the 19th century, with modern additions derived from European languages. The Jewish people living in Palestine developed a Hebrew-speaking culture. The poster above says, "For your own sake, and the sake of your children, learn Hebrew!" Hebrew became the main official language of the State of Israel when it was formed in 1948.

Modern Hebrew

Hebrew is written from right to left and is usually written without vowels, although vowel sounds were added to the text of the Hebrew Bible in the 6th century CE to make it easier to read. The first dictionary of modern Hebrew, compiled by Eliezer Ben-Yehuda, was published in 1908. In Israel today, new immigrants learn Hebrew at special schools.

א	'
ב	b
ג	v
ד	g
ה	d
ו	h
ז	w
ח	z
ט	ḥ
י	ṭ
כ	y
ל	k
מ	l
נ	m
ס	n
ע	s
פ	'
צ	p
ק	f
ר	ṣ
ש	q
ש	r
ת	ś
	sh
	t

A chart of the Hebrew alphabet showing the 22 letters, from top to bottom.

Origins of Judaism

The Jewish people believe they are descended from an ancient **Semitic** tribe that lived in the land of **Canaan**, which included most of modern Israel, Jordan, and Syria. In the second and third millennia BCE, there were several great centers of civilization in the Middle East; Canaan lay between them. Without doubt, the traditions of these civilizations had an influence on Judaism. Yet other people prayed to many gods, while Jews worshiped just one.

The snake goddess from the Minoan civilization of Crete (2000–1500 BCE). She contributed many characteristics to later Greek goddesses. The Greeks worshiped many gods, all of whom were considered to be immortal. They were thought to control various natural or social forces.

The Romans had household gods, called lares and penates, in the home. They made offerings and prayers to them. In Judaism, the home is also a place of worship.

BLACK SEA

CRETE

MEDITERRANEAN SEA

CANAAN

EGYPT

Early gods
The Egyptian gods, Anubis and Thoth (right,) weighed a dead person's heart to see if he or she had been good during their life. The Egyptians had many gods, some related to nature and others linked to ideas. Thoth was the god of wisdom, justice, and writing. Egypt played an important role in Middle Eastern history and is often mentioned in the Hebrew Bible.

Young cattle were worshiped in many parts of the ancient Near East. In the Bible, Moses smashed a figure like this because Jews were to worship only one God.

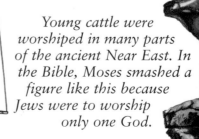

Early Canaanite religion
When the Jewish people came to Canaan, the Canaanite religion was basically a fertility cult. There were many gods and goddesses, linked to the different powers of the natural world. The chief god was El, creator of the world. His son was Baal (left), a weather god who brought the rains in the fall.

The cult of Mithras was practiced in ancient Persia. The most important Mithraic ceremony was the slaying of the bull.

Zoroastrianism
Zoroastrianism was an ancient Persian religion, founded by Zarathustra, who lived around 1200 BCE. He developed a religion based on the coming of a savior and a day of judgement, beliefs that were later absorbed by Judaism, Christianity, and Islam.

CASPIAN
SEA

MESOPOTAMIA

PERSIA

This map of the Middle East is from about the time of the emergence of the Jews, around 2000–1000 BCE. Among the most powerful civilizations were the Mesopotamians, Babylonians, and Egyptians. Later, the Greeks and Romans held power in the Middle East.

A ziggurat dedicated to the god Marduk.

This stela, associated with Hammurabi, King of Babylon (1792–50 BCE), is inscribed with laws relating to issues such as trade, tariffs, marriage, theft, and debt. Many of them are similar to the ones that Moses would later use.

Mesopotamia
The cities of Mesopotamia were all dedicated to a god or goddess. Many cities placed the temple to the divinity on the top of a platform called a **ziggurat**. According to the Mesopotamian people's creation story, Marduk formed Heaven and Earth from the bodies of his opponents after a conflict. The Mesopotamians also had myths of death and resurrection – and one about a great flood, similar to the Flood in Judaism.

From the Patriarchs to the Promised Land

Jewish people believe Abraham was the first Jew. In the first half of the second millennium BCE, Abraham left the Mesopotamian city of Ur and was commanded by God to move to the land of Canaan. His grandson, Jacob, had twelve sons, whose families became the twelve tribes of Israel. Several generations later, they were enslaved by the Egyptians, but were eventually led to freedom by Moses.

Stained-glass window showing Abraham. According to Genesis, God told Abraham to leave Ur, promising him he would be the father of a great nation, although he was 75 years old and had no children at that time.

After 40 years, the Israelites reached the Promised Land of Canaan. According to archaeologists, Canaan was gradually settled by a mixture of Israelite groups, some from Egypt.

After the great flood, Noah released a raven and a dove from the Ark. The book of Genesis says that God sent the flood to destroy the human race. Only Noah, his family, and one pair of each type of animal were spared.

Abraham and Isaac
Wanting to test Abraham's faith, God commanded him to sacrifice his first son Isaac. Abraham was willing to obey, but at the last minute God told him to sacrifice a ram instead. God then repeated his promise that Abraham would be the father of a great nation. Abraham's descendants settled in Canaan, but when famine threatened the region, Abraham's grandson Jacob took his family to the land of Egypt.

This early 15th-century panel shows Abraham ready to sacrifice Isaac.

Isaac's son Jacob dreamed that he saw angels climbing a ladder to Heaven, and he heard God promising that the land he lay on would always belong to him and his descendants. Years later, Jacob wrestled with an angel and changed Jacob's name to "Israel" (meaning one who strives with God.)

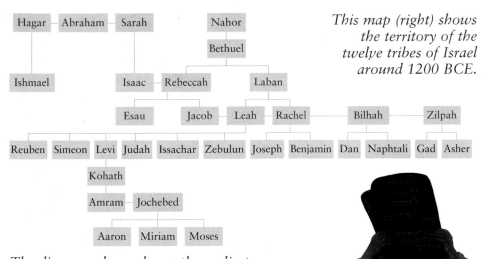

Hagar — Abraham — Sarah   Nahor

Bethuel

Ishmael   Isaac — Rebeccah — Laban

Esau   Jacob   Leah   Rachel   Bilhah   Zilpah

Reuben Simeon Levi Judah Issachar Zebulun Joseph Benjamin Dan Naphtali Gad Asher

Kohath

Amram — Jochebed

Aaron   Miriam   Moses

The diagram above shows the earliest Jewish people, from Abraham to Moses, and the twelve tribes of Israel.

This map (right) shows the territory of the twelve tribes of Israel around 1200 BCE.

Moses

Moses was an Israelite prophet and leader. Raised by an Egyptian princess in the pharaoh's court, when he found out he was an Israelite, he led the enslaved Jewish people out of Egypt to freedom.

In Deuteronomy, it is said that God spoke directly with Moses on Mount Sinai and Moses received God's teachings.

In the Book of Joshua it is said that the Israelites captured the city of Jericho and other cities in an impressive series of victories. However, it is likely that the Israelites gradually settled in Canaan, eventually becoming dominant.

Exodus

Moses and the Israelites on their 40-year journey through the desert from Egypt to the Promised Land. According to the story in Exodus, about 2 million people escaped from slavery. Although there is no historical evidence, it seems possible that many groups originally went to Egypt, and most of the tribes who eventually colonized Canaan may have been descended from them. There is evidence that some Israelite tribes did not go to Egypt at all.

The Hebrew Bible

Jewish people call the Hebrew Bible the Torah. In the narrow sense, the Torah is the first five books of the Christian Bible – the Old Testament – plus Nevi'im (Prophets) and Ketuvim (holy writings). Called the written Torah, or Tenakh, it includes the history of the Jews and their moral and legal code. The word "Torah" can also include the whole body of holy teachings that explain the Bible and guide Jews in their daily lives. These teachings are known as the oral Torah, or **Talmud**.

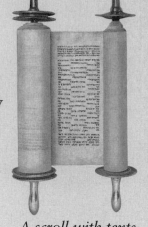

A scroll with texts from the Torah.

The ink pot found at Qumran indicates that the scribes of the Qumran community may have written the manuscripts found there.

Origin of the Torah

The traditional view is that God gave the Torah to Moses on Mount Sinai. We don't know who really wrote the Torah, but it seems to have been compiled from different sources. There are inconsistencies and contradictions between the stories, some are repeated, and there are stylistic differences that suggest different writers. In 1947, archeologists working at Qumran, on the shores of the Dead Sea, found some scrolls in terra-cotta jars. In 68 CE, the Essenes hid these scrolls in caves so they would not be destroyed by the Romans. They contain many books of the Hebrew Bible.

This chart illustrates the sections of the Hebrew Bible. The first five books are historical. They tell the story of mankind from Creation until Moses's death, just before the Israelites occupied Canaan. The next section, Nevi'im, tells how the Israelites conquered Canaan and lived there until Jerusalem was captured by the Babylonians and the Jews were exiled to Babylon. Ketuvim, the next section, contains varied writings, including what happened to the Jews during the Persian period (538 BCE to 333 BCE).

A professional scribe checks that a handwritten Torah scroll is perfect before it can be read in synagogue. There is a long tradition of scribal arts in Judaism.

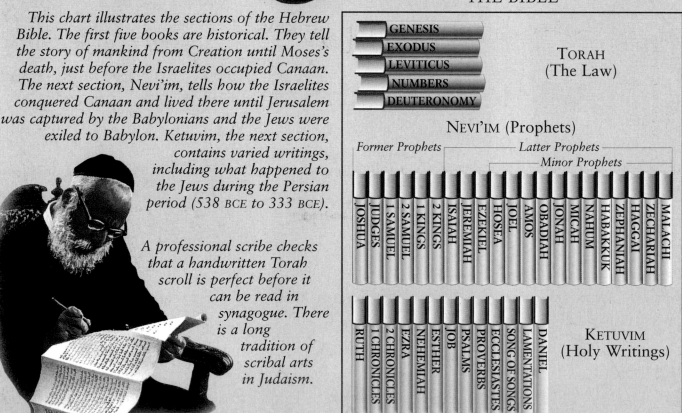

THE BIBLE

GENESIS
EXODUS
LEVITICUS
NUMBERS
DEUTERONOMY

TORAH
(The Law)

NEVI'IM (Prophets)

Former Prophets — Latter Prophets — Minor Prophets

JOSHUA, JUDGES, 1 SAMUEL, 2 SAMUEL, 1 KINGS, 2 KINGS, ISAIAH, JEREMIAH, EZEKIEL, HOSEA, JOEL, AMOS, OBADIAH, JONAH, MICAH, NAHUM, HABAKKUK, ZEPHANIAH, HAGGAI, ZECHARIAH, MALACHI

RUTH, 1 CHRONICLES, 2 CHRONICLES, EZRA, NEHEMIAH, ESTHER, JOB, PSALMS, PROVERBS, ECCLESIASTES, SONG OF SONGS, LAMENTATIONS, DANIEL

KETUVIM
(Holy Writings)

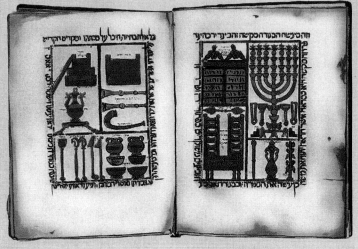

These pages come from an illuminated Hebrew Bible called the Perpignan Bible, written in southern France in the 13th century. The ritual objects of the Temple are painted in detail, and the name of each object appears next to it in Hebrew script.

The Torah scrolls are rolled on two wooden staves and bound with a decorative wrapper. In the Ashkenazi tradition, they are then covered with a mantle of embroidered material, as shown here. Sephardi Jews use a rigid case.

Sacred Scrolls

The Torah scroll is too sacred to touch with the hands, so it is held by handles, and a pointer called a yad (shown here) is used by the reader. As the letters are close together, the yad helps the reader to follow the words without the risk of smudging the carefully inscribed holy text.

Storing the Torah

This is a wooden case, in which Sephardi Jews keep the Torah. The Torah is at the heart of the Jewish religion. Obeying the Torah means following God's guidance. Jews believe they are special because God revealed the Torah to them. The reading of the Torah is a major part of worship in the synagogue.

David, King of the Israelites

King David, shown here in a 15th-century painting, is seen as a hero of Jewish history. Born a shepherd boy, he rose to become king in about 1000 BCE. According to the Talmud, David wrote most of the psalms in the Book of Psalms in Ketuvim, although the Talmud mentions ten other authors as well. The psalms are a collection of praises to God.

The Age of Kings

Before the Israelites had a monarchy, they were ruled by judges, charismatic leaders who arose when their people were threatened by enemies. The Bible shows that, by the 11th century BCE, this system was breaking down as the Israelites united as one nation. Their first king was Saul, a tragic figure who took his own life. He was followed by David, who expanded Israel's territory, and Solomon, who built the Temple in Jerusalem.

Above: Illustration from a Byzantine Psalter (c.950 CE) showing David with the prophet Nathan. David's affair with Bathsheba was condemned by Nathan (left), and David is shown repenting (right).

The Philistines

During the 11th century BCE, the Israelites were under threat from the Philistines, who were trying to extend their territory. This external threat was part of the reason that the Israelites united as one nation under King Saul (c.1029–1007 BCE). The Bible describes how King David broke the power of the Philistines; the Book of Samuel includes the romantic story of David, the brave, handsome youth who slayed the Philistine giant, Goliath.

A piece of Philistine pottery, thought to show a fertility goddess.

The Bible tells how the elderly Samuel was asked to appoint a new type of ruler, a king. The illustration below, from the Nuremberg Bible of 1483, shows Samuel anointing Saul.

King David

David, the second king of Israel (c.1000–967 BCE), expelled the Philistines and conquered Jerusalem. He extended his territory by defeating several neighboring peoples. Although portrayed in the Bible as a great hero, he was far from perfect. He fell in love with Bathsheba, the wife of one of his army officers, Uriah. After sending Uriah off to die in battle, David married Bathsheba.

This stela (right) written in Aramaic, is apparently the only reference to King David's dynasty apart from the Bible. The stela seems to record a victory by Hazael, a king of Aram, over Israel and Judah.

Kingdom of Israel and Judah
Vassal kingdoms
Solomon's empire

Damascus

PHOENICIA
Dan
Hazor
ARAM (SYRIA)
Acco
Dor
Megiddo
Ramoth-gilead
Beth-shan
Hepher
ISRAEL
Shechem
Jaffa
Shiloh
Balaath
Gezer
Beth-horon
AMMON
Jerusalem
Gaza
Hebron
JUDAH
Salt Sea
Beersheba
MOAB
Tamar
EDOM
Solomon's fortification or building project
Ezion-geber

The Israelite Empire

During the reigns of Saul and David, the empire of the Israelites was greatly expanded. Saul beat the Philistines, and David defeated the Moabites, Edomites, Ammonites, Syrians, and Phoenicians. All of their lands were incorporated into the Israelite Empire.

Left: A map of Israelite territories under the rule of Solomon.

Solomon's Rule

King Solomon (970–928 BCE) did not embark on any new battles with neighboring countries, and his reign was remembered as a time of peace when "Judah and Israel lived in safety, from Dan to Beersheba" (1 Kings 4.25). But he protected his kingdom from attack by stationing garrisons of chariots and cavalry in strategic places. Under Solomon, the Israelite Empire became an important international power, extending its influence with neighboring states by making diplomatic treaties.

A reconstruction of Jerusalem as it looked during the rule of King Solomon.

King Solomon's projects

Solomon doubled Jerusalem's size but the number of inhabitants (about 2,000) stayed the same. He did not expand the empire, but started many building projects, using forced labor. A new water supply system was built in Jerusalem, and Solomon built an enormous palace for himself.

A reconstruction of Solomon's Temple (below), the most important of his building projects. It was an impressive dwelling place for the nation's God.

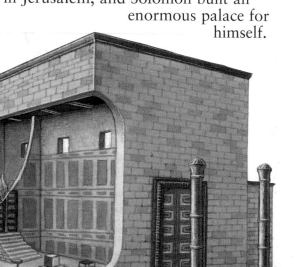

Above: The Ark of the Covenant, containing the Ten Commandments engraved in stone, was guarded by cherubs (like the one shown above) on either side, with their wings outstretched.

The Babylonian Period

With the death of King Solomon in 928 BCE, the kingdom of Israel split into two rival kingdoms: **Judah** in the south and Israel in the north. The Assyrians destroyed the kingdom of Israel in 722 BCE, and the ten tribes of Israel were dispersed forever. In 586 BCE, Judah was conquered by the Babylonians. The Jewish inhabitants went into exile in Babylon, where they remained for fifty years. In Babylon, they formed an organized Jewish community.

A clay tablet showing a Babylonian map of the world, dating from about 700 BCE. The round shape in the center is Babylonia.

An illustration of the gate to the city of Babylon.

Arrival in Babylon
When the Jewish exiles reached Babylon, they found a well-developed capital city, which stood on the Euphrates River, an important transport route. The exiles were devastated by the loss of Jerusalem, and the destruction of their Temple. Yet it is probable that their life in Babylon was quite prosperous.

The Hanging Gardens of Babylon
The Hanging Gardens were listed as one of the Seven Wonders of the World in the 2nd century BCE. Built within the walls of the royal palace, the gardens did not really hang, but were terraced roof gardens. They were irrigated with water from the Euphrates River. According to legend, King Nebuchadnezzar (ruled c.630–562 BCE), constructed the gardens for his wife, Amytis, who missed the greenery of her homeland, Media.

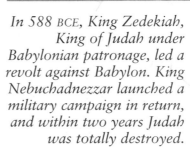

In 588 BCE, King Zedekiah, King of Judah under Babylonian patronage, led a revolt against Babylon. King Nebuchadnezzar launched a military campaign in return, and within two years Judah was totally destroyed.

This seal (right) belonged to a high official who served Jeroboam II. Jeroboam was King of Israel in the 8th century BCE, during the period in which the two kingdoms of former Israel had split apart.

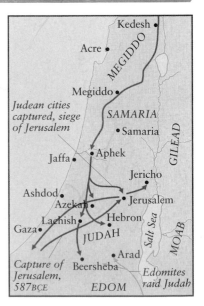

Kedesh

Acre

MEGIDDO

Megiddo

Judean cities captured, siege of Jerusalem

SAMARIA

Samaria

GILEAD

Jaffa

Aphek

Jericho

Ashdod

Jerusalem

Azekah

Hebron

Lachish

Salt Sea

Gaza

JUDAH

MOAB

Arad

Capture of Jerusalem, 587 BCE

Beersheba

Edomites raid Judah

EDOM

The story of Judith (left) appears in the Apocrypha – biblical books that are not accepted by all Christians as genuine. Judith was a rich Israelite woman, and it is recounted that she saved the town of Bethulia in Judah from Nebuchadnezzar's army. She captured his general, Holofernes, and cut off his head.

This painting by Rembrandt (right) shows the Prophet Jeremiah lamenting the destruction of Jerusalem in 586 BCE. It is believed that he prophesied the fall of Jerusalem and the Babylonian exile, and other events.

The Tower of Babel

In the story in Genesis, the Tower of Babel was built in an attempt to reach Heaven. God complicated the project by confusing the languages of the builders so that they could not understand each other. The description of the tower is probably based on the great ziggurat of Babylon, built by Nebuchadnezzar in the 6th century BCE. After Nebuchadnezzar destroyed Jerusalem, Babylon was described in the Bible as the embodiment of wickedness, a place doomed to destruction. However, the exile of the leading citizens of Judah to Babylon led to the city becoming a great Jewish intellectual center.

The Tower of Babel, *painted by Pieter Bruegel, 1563.*

Above: An illustration showing workers building the ziggurat in Babylon. The building had a base with five platforms above it, crowned by a temple to which the god was thought to descend.

Prophets, Priests, and Rabbis

The Prophets in the Hebrew Bible were people who communicated with God in a special way, and could act or speak on his behalf. Their main function was to maintain their nation's good relationship with God. They could also foretell the future. Prophets either served the needs of one locality or worked in an organized guild of prophets that moved around the country. There were also court prophets, who offered divine guidance to their king. The era of the great prophets was around 11th–6th century BCE. The Jewish priesthood dates from the 10th century BCE, and was most significant during the period of the Second Temple. After its destruction, rabbis replaced the priests as authorities on Jewish Law, but priests still retain certain key duties today.

The Prophet Amos

Amos was from Judah, but he prophesied in Israel, during the last days before its destruction in 721 BCE. He proclaimed judgement on Israel for its failure to follow divine laws, its corruption, and its cruel treatment of the poor. He foresaw Israel's demise. The final words of the Book of Amos foretold that Israel would be restored, but it is possible that someone else wrote this part.

Above: A painting of the Prophet Amos.

Above: Isaiah was an important prophet, 8th century BCE. The Book of Isaiah was later edited by disciples, but retains Isaiah's strong voice condemning social abuses of the rulers.

Micah

Micah was from Judah, but he prophesied against Samaria, the capital of Israel, so he must have been active before 721 BCE. Lots of later material was added to the collection of his prophecies. Like most prophets, Micah prophesied a mixture of doom and prosperity. He denounced Israel and Judah, but after Israel was destroyed, he said, it would rise again. Micah was the first prophet to speak of a future Messiah.

Right: A painting of Ezekiel in the Sistine Chapel, Rome.

The Prophet Micah, painted by Jan Van Eyck in 1432, in a cathedral in Ghent, Belgium.

Ezekiel

Ezekiel came from a priestly family in Jerusalem. He was taken as a captive to Babylonia in 597 BCE, where he was active as a prophet. He prophesied the destruction of Jerusalem, which occurred in 586 BCE.

Jonah

Jonah is one of the minor prophets. According to the Book of Jonah, God instructed him to go to Nineveh and prophesy disaster because of the city's wickedness. Jonah did not want to give the city the chance to repent and be spared. While traveling in the opposite direction to Nineveh, he jumped ship during a storm, confessing that it was his misdeeds that caused the storm. After being swallowed by a "great fish," he prayed for rescue and then finally went to Nineveh. He prophesied against the city, the citizens repented their wickedness, and Nineveh was saved.

Below: Illustration of Jonah in the whale's mouth.

Below: Painting of a priest by Titian.

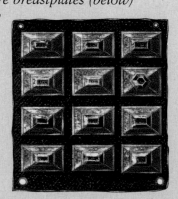

Above: Engraving of Daniel between two fierce lions.

The Book of Daniel

In the Hebrew Bible, the Book of Daniel is not in Nevi'im since it does not contain genuine prophecy. Although set in the 6th century BCE, during the Babylonian exile, it was probably written in the 2nd century BCE. One story tells how Daniel was thrown into a lions' den for refusing to worship King Nebuchadnezzar's golden idol, but God saved him.

Jewish priesthood

In biblical times, the priesthood was continued by the male descendants of Aaron, of the tribe of Levi. The cohanim (priests) had religious duties connected with the Temple, and certain privileges. After the Second Temple was destroyed, the priesthood became less important and rabbis replaced the cohanim as teachers. Many Cohanim today – those with surnames like Cohen or Kahn – pronounce blessings at festivals, among other duties.

Rabbis

Rabbis are teachers who study the Torah and apply it to daily life. They also lead services in synagogue and conduct weddings and funerals. Rabbis do community work, visit the sick and bereaved, and advise on spiritual matters.

High priests wore special clothing, like this blue tunic edged with gold bells (left). They also wore breastplates (below) decorated with twelve jewels that were engraved with the names of the twelve tribes of Israel.

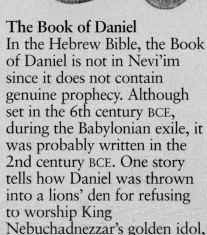

Left: A rabbi reading the Torah using a yad.

21

The Great Diaspora

In 539 BCE, King Cyrus of Persia conquered the mighty Babylonian Empire. In 538, he permitted the Jews to return to Judah. Most chose to stay in Babylon. Those who returned found their beloved Jerusalem in ruins, but they rebuilt it. By 322 BCE, Alexander the Great had conquered the Persian Empire; he and his successors promoted Greek culture, which was fiercely resisted by a section of the Jewish community. But it was the Romans after 63 BCE who finally defeated the Jews, and after 135 CE most were forced to disperse.

Soldiers of the Palace Guard in the Persian capital of Susa, during King Darius I's reign (522–486 BCE). The Persians were enlightened rulers, permitting exiles to return and allowing religious freedom.

(Above) A painting showing the Jews returning to Jerusalem.

The Cyrus Cylinder
The Cyrus Cylinder (right) records how Cyrus conquered Babylon and restored the gods to their home cities. Cyrus allowed many exiled populations to return to their homelands. The Jews were permitted to return to Jerusalem. Part of the Cyrus Proclamation reads: "The Lord God of heaven hath given me all the kingdoms of the earth; and he hath charged me to build him a house at Jerusalem ...Who is there among you of his people?... let him go up to Jerusalem."

The Return to Jerusalem
The Jews returned to Jerusalem in stages. The first occurred after King Cyrus's decree of 538 BCE, and was led by Zerubbabel. This was the main party of returning exiles, numbering about 50,000 people. It was mostly people from the poorer sections of Jewish society who chose to come back. In the following century, further returns were led by Ezra and Nehemiah.

This map (right) shows the route of the exiles' return to Jerusalem.

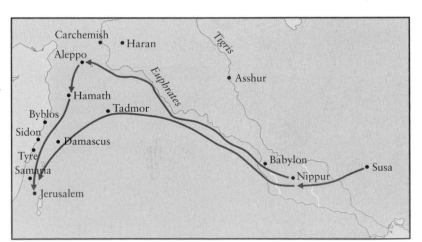

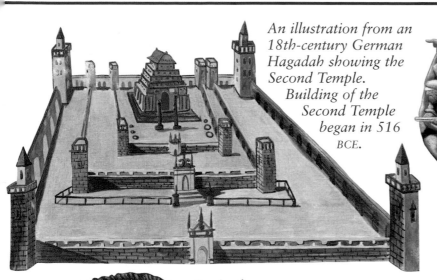

An illustration from an 18th-century German Hagadah showing the Second Temple. Building of the Second Temple began in 516 BCE.

Nehemiah (left) returned to Jerusalem in 445 BCE and became its governor. He reorganized the city's economy and arranged the reconstruction of its walls, laying the ground for Jerusalem's development.

Antiochus

Tensions between the Greek Empire after 332 BCE and the Jews of Judah (now called Judea) heightened when the Greek-Syrian king, Antiochus IV (175–163 BCE), tried to force the Jews to adopt Greek culture. This caused a revolt, led by Judah Maccabee, who succeeded in taking Jerusalem from Antiochus in 164 BCE and creating a Jewish state in Judea once more.

(Left) Mask of the Syrian king, Antiochus.

The Roman general, Pompey (above), gained control of Syria and Palestine, including Judea, in 63 BCE.

Roman rule

After Romans took control of Palestine, many Jews fled to Babylon, while others moved to Rome, Egypt, Persia, Spain, and other Middle East and North African countries. They lived under generally favorable conditions in Babylon and the Roman Empire.

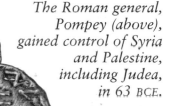

Coins minted by Jewish rebels (top, middle) and by the Romans (left) commemorating the two great Jewish revolts against harsh Roman rule in Palestine.

Below: Shown in a relief from the Arch of Titus (built in 81 CE), Roman soldiers are parading the menorah, raided from the Second Temple.

Jewish Revolts

In the First Revolt (66–73 CE) Jerusalem fell (70 CE) and the Temple was destroyed. After the Second Revolt (132–135 CE), many Jews left the country to live in the **Diaspora**.

Right: The map shows the Roman Empire at its greatest extent, in the 2nd century CE.

BRITAIN
GAUL
SPAIN
ITALY
DALMATIA
DACIA
Rome
GREECE
Carthage
Black Sea
Byzantium
ANATOLIA
Antioch
Mediterranean Sea
JUDAEA
Jerusalem
Leptis Magna
Alexandria
EGYPT

The Synagogue

A synagogue exists in every Jewish community. Its origin is not quite clear, but it seems that the synagogue became a place of worship after the destruction of the Second Temple in 70 CE. Modern synagogues are places of worship for the faithful, who can attend formal services up to three times a day. They are also a place for studying Judaism; there are usually classrooms. Most synagogues also have a hall that is used for celebrations and community events.

*In a synagogue, the scrolls of the Torah are kept in a cupboard called the **Ark** (right). It is positioned behind a curtain on the wall of the synagogue that faces Jerusalem. When the Ark's doors are opened, people stand up to show their respect for the Torah.*

A synagogue is usually rectangular, with seats on three sides. The fourth side faces Jerusalem. Orthodox synagogues have separate seating areas for men and women. In the center of the synagogue is the bimah, and the Ark is at the front.

Ner Tamid
Above the Ark in every synagogue, there is a perpetual light which never goes out. Called the ner tamid, it represents the menorah, the oil lamp of the Temple in Jerusalem. The Temple menorah had seven wicks, one of which burned continually. Near the ner tamid there is often a plaque with the Ten Commandments on it.

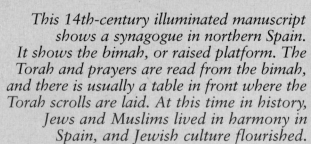

This 14th-century illuminated manuscript shows a synagogue in northern Spain. It shows the bimah, or raised platform. The Torah and prayers are read from the bimah, and there is usually a table in front where the Torah scrolls are laid. At this time in history, Jews and Muslims lived in harmony in Spain, and Jewish culture flourished.

The Tablets of the Law, containing the Ten Commandments, are at the top of the Ark, with a crown above them. Usually just the first phrase of each Commandment is shown.

Left: This curtain from Germany (1725) is made of velvet embroidered with gold thread, with other pieces of ornamental fabric sewn on, and it hangs outside the Ark. In Sephardi tradition, the curtain hangs inside.

Synagogue building

From the end of the 4th century onward, the Roman Empire, which ruled Palestine, passed laws prohibiting the building of new synagogues. Yet strangely, the 4th to the 7th centuries were a golden age for synagogue construction.

Right: A mosaic, (6th century CE), found in Bet-Shean Synagogue, Israel.

Jewish integration

Jewish communities made efforts to fit into the host countries in which they lived by adopting local cultural forms. Between the 16th and 18th centuries, Jews were gradually accepted back into western European society.

This synagogue in Strasbourg (1898) looks like a church from the outside. Its design shows the influence of the Romanesque and Gothic styles of the Middle Ages.

Above: A 6th-century mosaic floor from the synagogue in Ein-Gedi. Some of the synagogues built at this time were magnificent, imposing buildings, which could be seen from a great distance. The entrances of these synagogues faced Jerusalem, but there was no fixed place for the Torah Ark.

The Development of Judaism

After their defeat by the Romans in 135 CE, the Jewish people moved all over the world. They continued to migrate, depending on the degree of persecution they faced in different places. After the western European countries expelled their Jewish populations between the 13th and 15th centuries, two main groups of Jews formed. The Sephardim (meaning "Spanish") were forced out of Spain and they moved to Muslim lands such as the Ottoman Empire. The Ashkenazim (meaning "Germans") were expelled from Germany and settled in Poland. Jewish communities developed in many countries, including China, India, and Ethiopia.

Ashkenazi culture
11th century
14th century
16th century
Sephardim culture

Watercolor of a Jewish man in 1714 in the Ottoman Empire (above), where Jews were involved in the medical profession.

Right: The occupations of Ashkenazi Jews in Poland, based on a 13th-century source. Jews maintained their religious traditions, methods of teaching, and social structure in Poland.

Above: Map showing the expansion of Ashkenazi culture. Jews settled in Poland at the same time as German settlement grew there.

Cobbler

Weaver

Above: This map shows the spoken languages of the Jews. These were usually developed by combining the local language with Hebrew and Aramaic, and writing it in Hebrew script. Most Jewish tongues have died out, but Ladino and Yiddish have survived to this day.

Smith

Marranos

In 1497 Portugal adopted a policy of converting Jews to Christianity instead of expelling them. The "Conversos" (converts), or Marranos, as they became known, continued to practice Judaism in private. In the 17th century, many Marranos went to Amsterdam, where they could practice their religion freely. Amsterdam became an important center for Judaism. Manasseh ben Israel, a Marrano, founded the city's first printing press in 1626.

Above: An ex-libris – a book plate bearing the owner's name pasted into a book – belonging to Manasseh ben Israel.

Ethiopian Jews

The Ethiopian Jews call themselves Beta Israel, but they are known as Falashas (foreigners). Most modern scholars believe that their origins lie in Jewish cultural influences that reached Ethiopia between the 7th century BCE and the 4th century CE. They retained their autonomy over many centuries, but were only recognized as proper Jews in 1973.

Above: An amulet from Ethiopia, early 20th century.

(Right) A tenth-century inscription in Tamil concerning the Jews of Malabar.

(Above) Jewish woman with her daughter in Cochin, India in 1983, preparing matzah.

Indian Jews

There are two groups of Indian Jews. The Bene Israel believe they reached India in the 2nd century BCE, although this has not been proven. They observed the **Sabbath** and followed the Jewish dietary laws. The earliest evidence of the second group, the Jews of Kerala, dates from c.1000 CE.

Jews in China

Jewish traders reached China perhaps as early as the second century BCE. The only real Jewish community there was in Kaifeng, eastern China, and dated from the 11th century CE when about 1,000 Jews from Persia or India settled there. They built a synagogue in 1163. In 1605 a Jesuit missionary, Matteo Ricci, met a man from Kaifeng who told him about the Jews of Kaifeng. He said they had a Hebrew Torah in their synagogue, did not eat pork, and circumcised their sons. Yet the only concrete evidence of the Kaifeng Jews is provided by some prayer books found in the 19th century. Over the years the community became integrated with the local Chinese people, and had almost disappeared by the 19th century.

Above: A scroll of the book of Esther from Kaifeng in China.

Left: A synagogue in Kaifeng, reconstructed to show how it looked in the 18th century.

Sacred Writings

The study of the sacred writings is essential to Judaism. As well as the Hebrew Bible, there are writings about the halakhot, or Jewish laws, called the **Mishnah**. This was written down in about 200 CE to ensure that Jews remembered the laws. The Mishnah and the rabbis' comments on it together form the Talmud. Alongside the Talmud, the **Midrash** gives in-depth explanations about the Talmud. The **Kabbalah** is a collection of Jewish mystical knowledge.

Above: The cover of the Babylonian Talmud.

The Talmud

The Talmud is made up of the Mishnah – the Jewish laws divided into six sections – plus the commentaries on them by rabbis, known as the Gemara. Two versions of the Talmud were made. The first was the Jerusalem Talmud, compiled in c.400 CE. The other was the Babylonian Talmud, from c.550 CE. The Babylonian one became the most important and is now known simply as the Talmud.

Left: An illuminated page of a Pesach Hagadah (Barcelona, 1350).

Agadah

Agadah, meaning "telling," is a traditional way of examining the stories in the Bible by explaining the words used and interpreting the meaning. From the first century, people began writing down the Agadot (plural of Agadah) and these works became known as the Midrash.

The Mishneh Torah

The Mishneh Torah was written by Maimonides. It was a legal code with all of rabbinic Jewish law organized into a clear, logical framework. Included was a discussion of subjects such as the nature of God and his divine attributes, religious language, and the foundation of ethics. Maimonides wanted Jewish law to be accessible to everyone, not just scholars.

Left: Moses ben Maimon, known as Maimonides (1138–1204) was a leading medieval philosopher, he argued that the way God was described as a human in the Bible was not supposed to be understood literally.

Below: Illuminated page from the Mishneh Torah.

The Book of Splendor

Kabbalah means "that which is received." It is a study of the secrets of the Torah. Kabbalistic writings explain how God created the universe, the ways he reveals himself, and his relationship with human beings. Mostly written by Rabbi Moses de León (1250–1305), the Zohar – or Book of Splendor – is the most influential Kabbalistic text.

Left: The frontispiece of the first edition of the Sefer ha-Zohar – Book of Splendor – late 13th century.

The Book of Splendor describes ten sefirot, the attributes of God from which he created the universe. Here, they are shown as the branches of a tree. From top to bottom, right to left, they are: Supreme Crown, Wisdom, Intelligence, Greatness, Power, Beauty, Endurance, Majesty, Foundation, and Kingdom.

The Septuagint

The Septuagint was the first translation of the Old Testament from the original Hebrew into Greek. The translation was done between the 3rd and the 2nd century BCE in Egypt.

The sefirot

The sefirot (attributes of God) can be ordered and represented as points on a tree or a branched candlestick. The first three sefirot represent the intellectual realm of the divine. The second three reflect moral power. The next three represent the forces of nature, and the tenth is the channel between the divine and the material world. The Zohar stresses that human action could have a real effect on the higher world. Through serving God, people could be unified with him, and they could also repair the disharmony of the world.

Amulets

Amulets are charms against evil. Jewish amulets often contain religious sayings to recite, or symbols of Jewish religious identity. Amulets form a common part of Jewish mysticism, especially those containing sacred writings. However, Jewish people do not believe that such objects themselves have spiritual powers. They are simply containers for the word of God and are worn as constant reminders of people's obligations toward the Divine Power.

This amulet from Yemen was designed to be worn around the neck.

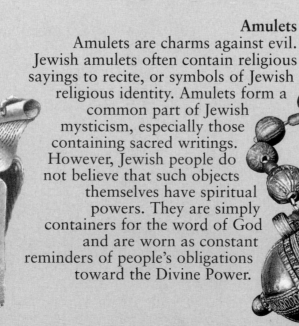

29

Centuries of Persecution

Throughout history, the Jewish people have been persecuted for having a different religion and culture to the majority. During the Middle Ages, they were tolerated under Islamic rule, although there were periods of harsh treatment. The Crusades – Christian military expeditions to recover the Holy Land – encouraged anti-Semitic violence, and between the 13th and 15th centuries, western European countries expelled their Jewish populations. Many refugees fled to eastern Europe. In the 19th century, Jews were recognized as equal citizens in most of Europe, but in Russia, Poland, and Romania they suffered under vicious persecution.

A 15th-century miniature showing the massacre of Jews. On their way to the Holy Land, the Crusaders murdered Jews, who preferred being burnt at the stake to being forced to become Christians.

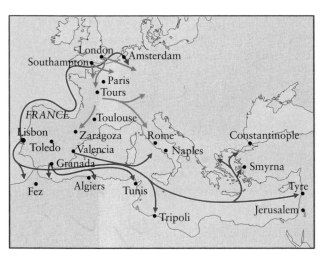

Map showing the movement of Jews after they were expelled from England, Spain, and France.

Expulsions of Jews
→ 1290
→ 1391
→ 1394
→ 1492–97

Wandering Jew puppet; for failing to allow the cross-carrying Jesus to rest against his house, the mythical Jew was to wander forever.

The Spanish Inquisition

In 1478, Pope Sixtus IV gave permission to the Spanish monarchs, Ferdinand and Isabela, to establish a new Inquisition in Spain. The inquisitors were to check whether Conversos (Jews who had converted to Christianity) had become genuine Christians. In the medieval era, Christians saw Jews as a threat to the community to be expelled or massacred. Conversion alone could save them.

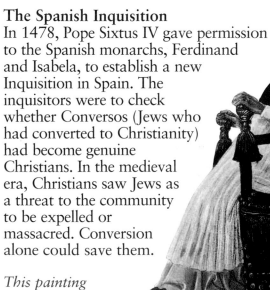

This painting shows Pope Sixtus IV in 1477.

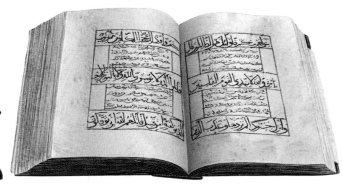

Muslim rule

Between the 15th and 19th centuries, many Jewish communities lived under Muslim rule, mainly in the Ottoman Empire. Mostly they were tolerated subjects, although they endured restrictions; for example, they were not allowed to own land. Yet harsh laws against Jews were passed in Shi'ite Muslim countries, such as in Persia from 1507–1736.

Polish Jews

In 17th-century Poland, Jews were mostly traders. They also administered estates for the Polish nobility under the arenda system, thus becoming hated by the Polish peasants. In 1648–49 a huge peasant and Cossack revolt destroyed many Jewish communities; 6,000 Jews were massacred in the community of Nemirov alone.

Above: An arenda jug for alcohol, shaped as a Jewish innkeeper, from Poland, 17th century.

Right: An anti-Semitic Russian cartoon showing a Jew being mocked by a judge, from the late 19th century. In Russia, laws were passed to try to make Jews give up their culture. Jewish men had to serve 25 years in the army; this was to weaken their ties to their communities.

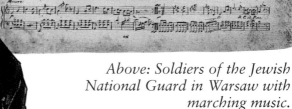

Above: Soldiers of the Jewish National Guard in Warsaw with marching music.

Poland

Jewish soldiers in Poland took part in the Polish rebellion against Russian rule in 1830–31, in the hope that it would save them from Nicholas I's cruel regime, under which Jews were confined to one area, and forced into military service.

Below: Early 20th-century painting showing US Jews welcoming their eastern European brethren. Between 1880 and 1920, over a third of eastern European Jews left their homes; 90 percent moved to the USA.

Right: A poster made by an American Jewish aid organization c.1915.

Jewish immigrants

The new Jewish immigrants tended to live in poor areas. They worked extremely hard in poor conditions to establish themselves in the garment trade, food production, and the construction industry. In the 1890s, anti-Semitism began to grow. The white Christian community resented the masses of poor immigrants with their different way of life. A campaign led to laws being passed in 1921–24 that limited immigration and showed preference for the "Nordic race."

Stages of Life

The various ceremonies that mark the stages in a Jewish lifetime are part of Jewish identity. Throughout history, a person born in the Jewish community would expect to grow up in that environment, marry and raise a Jewish family, and be buried with Jewish rituals. Each rite of passage, from the blessing of a baby to the lighting of the yahrzeit candle to remember the dead, has its own commandments to follow, reminding people of their duties to God.

A 19th-century cradle from Moravia. A child born to a Jewish mother is considered to be a Jew. Jewish baby girls have a naming ceremony in synagogue and boys are circumcised.

*Left: Instruments used for **circumcision**.*

Bar mitzvah

When a boy is 13 years old, he has a bar mitzvah ceremony to mark his entry into adulthood. The boy is called up in synagogue to read from the Torah for the first time. Friends and relatives attend to hear him read, and a celebration usually follows.

Circumcision

Circumcision is the removal of the foreskin from the penis. Boys are usually circumcised when they are eight days old and a celebration is held afterward. Circumcision marks the boy's entry into the covenant between God and the Jewish people.

Extended family

The extended family is important in Jewish culture, and young people are taught from an early age to respect their elders for their knowledge, and also because it is right to do so. For Jews, tzedaka – giving charity to those in need – is fundamental, and charity begins with close relatives. In Jewish communities, the elderly have always received special treatment. The directive "Honor your father and mother" (Exodus 20:12) is taken to mean respect for any elderly person.

Left: An elderly Jewish man with his grandson.

Above: A girl at her bat mitzvah ceremony, which marks her entry into womanhood at the age of 12.

Ketubah

A ketubah is a binding agreement between two Jewish people when they marry. It is usually a statement of the husband's intention to care for his wife. The reading of the ketubah is part of the marriage ceremony. Sometimes it is translated into the local language.

Right: A ketubah, a marriage contract, which is usually written in Aramaic.

Below: A jug for purifying a dead person's body before burial.

Marriage

Wedding ceremonies take place under a huppah, a canopy held up by four poles. This symbolizes the couple's home, but it is open on all sides to show that they are not separated from the community. Ideally the huppah is outdoors, but it can be in a home or synagogue. Blessings are said over wine, and the groom places a ring over his bride's finger. The ketubah is read out and seven blessings are recited. The groom also breaks a glass with his foot as a reminder of the destruction of the Temple.

Right: Celebrating the newly married couple.

Death

The death of a Jewish person is surrounded by rituals. For a week after a funeral, the family sits shiva (meaning "seven"). Mourners gather in one of their homes and visitors come to pray with them. Within a year, a headstone is placed at the grave. On each anniversary of the death a yahrzeit candle is lit and prayers are said for the dead person.

Below: A painting showing mourners carrying a dead person to be buried.

Burial

When Jewish people die, they are buried quickly, within 24 hours if possible. Jewish law forbids cremation, although it is acceptable in some Reform communities. The funeral is short; after a few prayers and a speech about the dead person, the burial takes place.

Pogroms and the Holocaust

During the Middle Ages, hatred of the Jews was based on their religion. By the mid-19th century, most European countries had given Jews citizenship and religious freedom. But a new form of anti-Semitism arose, based on Jews' so-called "racial" differences. This prejudice was adopted by the rising Nationalist movements, which viewed the Jews as outsiders who did not fit into the national identity and undermined nation states. Nazis in Germany in the 20th century believed that Jews should be exterminated. This hatred culminated in the Holocaust and the deaths of huge numbers of European Jews.

Above: This painting by Maurice Minkowsky (1880–1930) is entitled After the Pogrom.

Pogroms

In Russia, anti-Semitism became official policy after 1881, with restrictions adopted on rights of residence in the Jewish areas and jobs that Jews could do. The government wanted to scapegoat the Jews for Russia's problems, and there was already widespread anti-Semitism. **Pogroms** – massacres of Jews – occurred in 1881–4. The police did not stop the killing and looting. Pogroms also occurred in 1903–06 and 1917–21, during the periods of revolution.

Below: Jewish woman's passport in Nazi Germany.

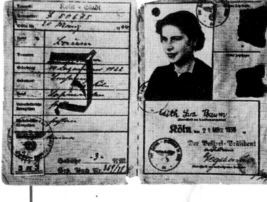

This painting shows Albert Einstein (1879–1955) among other German Jews leaving Germany in 1932.

Germany

Once Hitler came to power in 1933, many Jews tried to leave Germany. But the USA and western European countries were prepared to take only a certain number of immigrants. Some desperate families sent their children abroad alone. Most Jews were forced to stay.

Polish Jews

After the Nazis occupied Poland in 1939, they confined the Jews to sealed ghettos. Suffering from overcrowding and poor food supplies, ghetto communities struggled together to survive.

Above: A banknote issued in the Theresienstadt ghetto, Poland.

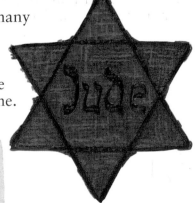

Above: The Star of David, which all Jews living under Nazi rule were forced to sew onto their clothing so that everyone knew they were Jewish.

Left: This monument commemorates the Warsaw Ghetto Uprising (April to July 1943).

Right: Suitcases belonging to Jewish people who had been deported to the central extermination center for western Europe, Auschwitz. Once they arrived at the camp, the prisoners had all their possessions taken away.

Concentration camps

The Nazis had two methods of exterminating Jews. Mobile killing units – the Einsatzgruppen – killed Jews near where they lived. Then, in 1941, concentration camps were built for the extermination of people the Nazis did not want living in their society. Jews, gypsies, blacks, homosexuals, and disabled people were rounded up and transported to these death camps in cattle trucks. Once there, the young and healthy were selected for hard labor, while the others were stripped and murdered in purpose-built gas chambers.

The Warsaw Ghetto Uprising

This uprising, in which Jewish fighters resisted the Nazis almost to the last person, was one of many brave uprisings against the Nazis, including several in concentration camps. None had a real chance of success.

Death camp survivors

The victory of the Allied forces over Germany came too late for the Jewish people. The Nazis continued to murder Jews until the last moment. Entering the death camps, the Allied soldiers found a few thousand survivors. They were living skeletons, barely alive. Many of them died shortly after their liberation.

Left: Survivors of Dachau concentration camp, newly liberated by US forces in April 1945.

Above: The entrance to a concentration camp, with the slogan "Freedom through work."

USSR

Jewish cultural identity was suppressed in the USSR. A campaign of persecution reached its peak during 1948–53; many intellectuals were imprisoned or shot.

Right: Joseph Stalin, Soviet leader, 1927–53.

The Jewish Calendar

Judaism has many festivals and holy days throughout the year. Some are major ones, when Jews stop their normal daily activities to spend time with their families and in prayer. Others are less significant, and daily life continues. There are two main types of festival. Festivals such as Hanukkah commemorate historical events when God helped the Jewish people through miracles. Other holy days, such as Shabbat and the New Year for Trees, celebrate God's role as the creator of nature. Some festivals fit into both categories. Yet Yom Kippur and Simchat Torah fit neither; they concern people's relationships with God and other people.

Rosh Hashanah/Yom Kippur
The **shofar**, made from a ram's horn, is blown in synagogue on Rosh Hashanah, the start of a ten-day period when Jews think about what they have done wrong over the past year. This ends at Yom Kippur, the Day of Atonement. People fast for 25 hours and go to synagogue to pray for forgiveness. The shofar is blown to call the people before God.

This chart shows the Jewish calendar. It uses natural months, 29 or 30 days long, which stretch from new moon to new moon. To use up the extra days, some years have a "leap month" to keep festivals in the right seasons. All festivals start at sunset, which is the start of the new day. Each festival has its own set of special commandments, prohibitions, and special foods to be prepared and enjoyed.

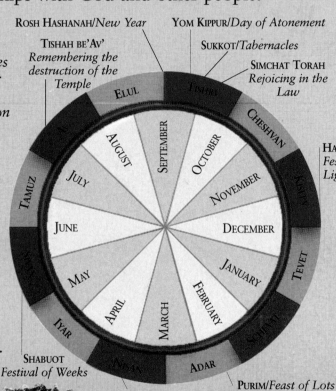

ROSH HASHANAH/*New Year*
YOM KIPPUR/*Day of Atonement*
TISHAH be'Av'/*Remembering the destruction of the Temple*
SUKKOT/*Tabernacles*
SIMCHAT TORAH/*Rejoicing in the Law*

HANUKKAH/*Festival of Lights*

SHABUOT/*Festival of Weeks*
PESACH/*Passover*
PURIM/*Feast of Lots*

ELUL
TISHRI
AV
CHESHVAN
TAMUZ
KISLEV
SIVAN
TEVET
IYAR
SHEVAT
NISAN
ADAR

AUGUST
SEPTEMBER
OCTOBER
JULY
NOVEMBER
JUNE
DECEMBER
MAY
JANUARY
APRIL
FEBRUARY
MARCH

A sukkah on a gondola in Venice, Italy. Sukkot commemorates the time when the Israelites lived in the desert in temporary shelters on their way to the Promised Land. At Sukkot, Jews build a sukkah, an outdoor shelter, and eat their meals there for seven days.

Simchat Torah
At the end of Sukkot comes Simchat Torah, "the joy of the Torah." The festival celebrates the end of the reading of the Torah, which then starts again. People parade the Torah around the synagogue and out in the streets. There is much singing and dancing as people rejoice in the love of their holy book.

Hanukkah

Hanukkah celebrates the Maccabees' revolt in 164 BCE. When the Maccabees relit the Temple lights, they found only enough oil to last one day, but miraculously it burned for eight days. At Hanukkah, one candle is lit the first night, two the second, and so on up to eight.

Right: Purim scroll of the Book of Esther.

Purim

Purim commemorates the time in the 5th century BCE when Esther, the Jewish wife of the King of Persia, saved her people from Haman, an official who planned to kill all the Jews. The book of Esther is read aloud and children shake rattles when Haman's name is mentioned. Purim is also marked with dress up parties.

Celebrating Pesach with a family meal.

Left: A Seder plate, to hold symbolic foods during Pesach.

Pesach

At Pesach (Passover), Jews celebrate the escape from slavery in Egypt. Families hold a Seder meal, at which the Hagadah (the story of the Exodus) is read. Seder plates have sections for symbolic foods: bitter herbs recall slavery; an egg and a lamb's shank bone stand for ritual sacrifice; salt water represents the Israelites' tears; haroseth (sweet nut and fruit paste) is a reminder of the mortar Jews mixed for building work. A dry cracker called matzah is eaten to show humility and recall the haste of the Israelites' flight from Egypt.

A boy reading from the Torah.

Shabuot

Shabuot celebrates the day that Moses received the Torah from God. It is also a harvest festival. People study the Torah and decorate synagogues with flowers.

A monument in Carpi, Italy, covered with names of Italian Jews who died in the Holocaust. Tishah Be'Av, the anniversary of the destruction of the First Temple, is a day of fasting and mourning for all Jewish tragedies.

The Founding of Israel

Constant persecution in 19th-century eastern Europe prompted a group of Jews to start the **Zionist** movement – they aimed to establish a Jewish homeland in Palestine. With Zionist support, many Jews migrated there. In 1947, the United Nations planned to divide the country into separate parts for Palestinians and Jews. This angered the Palestinians and war broke out. The State of Israel was declared on May 14, 1948, and Israel won the war. Since then, Israel has fought several wars with the neighboring Arab countries, and the conflict with the Palestinians remains unresolved.

Portrait of Theodor Herzl (1860–1904).

Theodor Herzl

Born in Hungary, Herzl came to believe that anti-Semitism in the Diaspora could not be stopped. In 1897 he founded the Zionist movement, which campaigned for a Jewish homeland in Palestine. Herzl devoted himself to building up international support for Zionism.

This poster shows three Zionist leaders. From left: Max Nordau, Theodor Herzl, and Professor Mandelstamm. The scenes beneath them show the Zionist ideals of settling in Israel and farming the land, and being near the Wailing Wall (the remains of the Second Temple in Jerusalem).

Zionism

Zionism was an international campaign, drawing on support from foreign governments and Jewish communities all over the world.

Left: A young woman waving the Zionist flag, which incorporates the Star of David. The Zionists called their ancient homeland Eretz Israel – the Land of Israel.

David Ben-Gurion (left) (1886–1973) was born in Poland and emigrated to Palestine in 1906. An active Zionist, he led the struggle for a Jewish state in the 1940s and became its first prime minister in 1948.

Below: An American Zionist poster.

Left: This Jewish National Fund poster from the 1930s is written in Hebrew, Yiddish and Polish. It says "Let us redeem the Jezreel Valley."

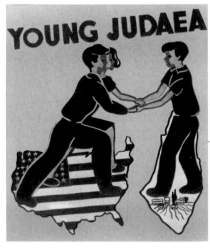

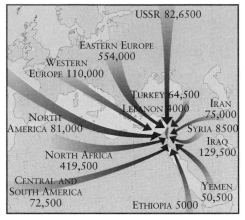

On May 15, 1948, the day after the State of Israel was declared, the neighboring Arab countries declared war. By January 1949, Israel had won more territory.

USSR 82,6500
EASTERN EUROPE 554,000
WESTERN EUROPE 110,000
TURKEY 64,500
LEBANON 4000
IRAN 75,000
NORTH AMERICA 81,000
SYRIA 8500
IRAQ 129,500
NORTH AFRICA 419,500
CENTRAL AND SOUTH AMERICA 72,500
YEMEN 50,500
ETHIOPIA 5000

Map showing the huge number of immigrants who moved to Israel from around the world, 1948–1996. Yet about 750,000 Palestinians were forced to flee in 1948.

Below: Rabbi Shlomo Goren, chief rabbi of the Israeli army, blowing the shofar on Mount Zion after the Six-Day War.

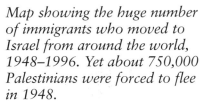

Below: Israeli New Year greeting card celebrating Israel's victory in the Six-Day War against the Arab countries. It shows two military leaders, Moshe Dayan (left) and Yitzhak Rabin.

The Six–Day War

During the Six-Day War in 1967, Israel occupied the Egyptian Sinai and Gaza Strip, the Syrian Golan Heights, and Jordanian Jerusalem and the West Bank. These areas held large Arab populations who did not want to be ruled by Israel, creating new conflicts.

Below: Map showing territorial changes after the Israeli–Arab wars of 1949, 1967, and 1973.

Golda Meir

Golda Meir (1898–1978) emigrated to Palestine in 1921 and was a leading Zionist activist. Elected to the Israeli Knesset (parliament) in 1949, she became prime minister in 1969. Her efforts to forge a peace settlement were halted by the Yom Kippur War of 1973. Israel's lack of readiness for war shocked the nation and Meir resigned in 1974.

Palestine

From the Palestinian point of view, Israel now occupies all of their country. Among Israelis, some believe that it is crucial to maintain control of the entire area, while others want to return territory to the Palestinians in order to achieve peace.

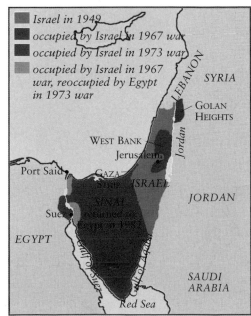

Israel in 1949
occupied by Israel in 1967 war
occupied by Israel in 1973 war
occupied by Israel in 1967 war, reoccupied by Egypt in 1973 war

LEBANON
SYRIA
GOLAN HEIGHTS
WEST BANK
Jerusalem
Jordan
Port Said
GAZA STRIP
ISRAEL
JORDAN
Suez
SINAI *returned to Egypt in 1982*
EGYPT
Gulf of Suez
Gulf of Aqaba
SAUDI ARABIA
Red Sea

Life and Worship

Religion affects all aspects of Jewish life. There are rituals with prayers for many daily activities – from getting up in the morning to going to bed at night. Jewish people believe that they should remember God in everything they do. In the Talmud, eating without first making a blessing over the meal is compared to robbing God of his property. Jews are permitted to enjoy the good things in life, such as delicious meals, joyous weddings, and happy children, but they must always thank God for them.

A mezuzah, which is usually fixed to every doorpost in a Jewish home. Traditionally, Jews touch their fingers to their lips and then to the mezuzah on the front door when they enter or leave the house. The mezuzah is a constant reminder to serve God.

The ritual of washing for purification is different from washing for cleanliness. It is a symbol of religious purity. Worshipers always wash their hands before prayer. They wash them before eating because the meal is a blessing from God.

Tallit and tefillin
A man wearing a tallit, a large, four-cornered robe, and tefillin, two black leather boxes wrapped around the head and arm. These are worn by men for morning prayers. The tefillin contain parchment scrolls with passages from the Bible. One box points to the heart, the other is bound to the head; they remind the wearer to serve God with his heart and mind.

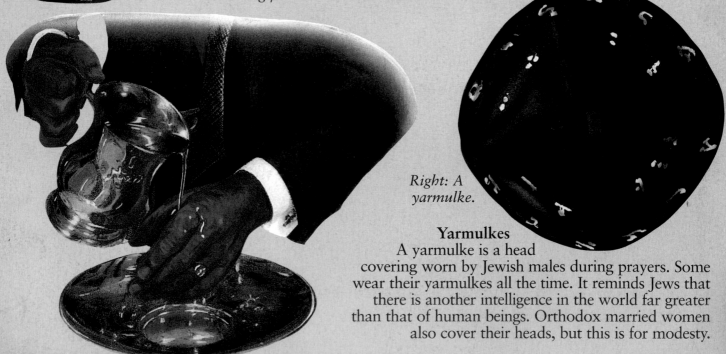

Right: A yarmulke.

Yarmulkes
A yarmulke is a head covering worn by Jewish males during prayers. Some wear their yarmulkes all the time. It reminds Jews that there is another intelligence in the world far greater than that of human beings. Orthodox married women also cover their heads, but this is for modesty.

Kosher food

Practicing Jews eat only **kosher** foods which they are permitted to eat under the laws of kashrut. Most raw foods, except for meat, which must be prepared in a special way, can be bought anywhere. But ready-cooked foods, such as those in the picture, may have been made using non-kosher ingredients, so Jews will buy them from a kosher shop.

Left: A woman sells food at a Kosher food counter.

Left: An incense burner. The smoke produced by the incense is symbolic of prayer. The inscription at the bottom reads "In heaven."

Meat

Dating back to the Torah, the laws defining which meats could be eaten may have been based on food hygiene. Nowadays, they are not observed for hygienic reasons; they are followed because to be holy involves eating meat only from certain animals.

Below: This 15th-century Italian illustration from a Hebrew law code shows the ritual killing of fowl and oxen.

Shabbat

On Friday night Shabbat begins, and the Jewish family gathers for a special meal. The mother lights two candles at sunset and says a blessing to welcome in Shabbat. At mealtime, she says a blessing of thanks over the challah (a festive bread) before the family eats.

Left: The Shabbat table, with candles, challah, and wine.

Wine

Kiddush, a prayer sanctifying Shabbat and festival days, is usually recited over a goblet of wine. At the Shabbat table, sweet wine is blessed and drunk by the family before the meal begins.

Right: A silver goblet for holding wine for use in blessings.

Judaism Today

Orthodox students studying in a yeshiva, an academy for the study of the Talmud.

There are Jews living all over the world, and their lifestyles are incredibly diverse. Between those who practice their religion, there are huge differences. Orthodox tradition teaches that the Torah was given by God and can never change; Orthodox Jews follow the Torah closely. Reform Jews believe that the Torah can be adapted to reflect modern times. Conservative Jews believe that the Torah was given by God, but that the practice of Judaism can change. Other sections of the community are proud to be Jewish, but they are not religious at all.

Studying the Talmud

Traditionally, young men study in pairs, examining the text and discussing it in Yiddish. Some continue to study and become rabbis or teachers, while others will later find a secular job.

Hasidic Jews in festive clothes in Jerusalem.

A Reform rabbi (below).

Hasidic Jews

The Hasidic tradition arose in eastern Europe in the 18th century. Hasidic Jews are intensely Orthodox and live in separate communities where they can live and work together, following their own customs. Their style of worship stresses enthusiasm and joy in their devotion to God.

A Jewish butcher at work.

Above: A Hasidic boy with the customary black hat and side-curls. Men and older boys wear black suits and white shirts. Women dress modestly in long, high-necked dresses; married women always keep their heads covered.

Reform Jews

Reform Jews do not follow the Torah exactly and have adapted their religious practice to modern life. In synagogue, men and women sit together, and some Reform synagogues have women rabbis. Children of a Jewish and a non-Jewish parent are accepted as Jews if they identify with the Jewish faith.

Jewish Food

All blood must be removed from meat before it can be consumed. Judaism has food laws, called kashrut, that govern which foods can be eaten and how meat is prepared. Jews may eat land animals that chew the cud and have cloven hooves, and fish with fins and scales. They must not eat meat and dairy products together. Orthodox Jews only eat in restaurants where all the rules are observed, but Reform Jews are less strict about kashrut.

Left: Pope John Paul II with Chief Rabbi Elio Toaff, Rome, 1986 – the first visit of a pope to a synagogue.

Judaism and Catholicism

There has always been tension between Judaism and Catholicism. The church has seen the Jews as the killers of Christ. During the Second World War, few Catholic figures stood out against the Holocaust. Since then, relations have improved and there is a growing mood of fellowship between Catholics and Jews.

*Above: This poster encourages American Jewish students to spend time on a **kibbutz**. A kibbutz is an Israeli community where volunteers can live and work for a while. Jewish volunteers often study Hebrew too.*

Right: A demonstration outside UN headquarters, New York in 1979 to oppose a UN resolution equating Zionism with racism. Many diaspora Jews defend Israel from criticism and provide financial support, but condemn certain actions, such as its treatment of Palestinians.

The Israeli Army

Ever since the State of Israel was established, it has been a heavily armed country. The army exercises control within Israel and in the territories under Israeli rule, and is always on alert to protect the country's borders. All men and women, with few exceptions, undertake military service.

An Israeli soldier.

Below: President Bill Clinton with Yitzhak Rabin (1922–1995) and Yasser Arafat (1929–) agreeing to a peace settlement in 1993 under which Palestinians were to be granted self-governing areas. The peace process did not progress as planned, and in 2000 a renewed Palestinian uprising against Israeli rule broke out.

Below: US film director Steven Spielberg, who made Schindler's List (1993), an epic film about the Holocaust. There are many world-famous Jewish musicians, writers, and actors, making an enormous contribution to the cultures of the countries where they live.

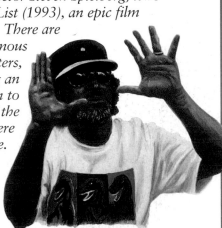

GLOSSARY

Ark: An ornamental cupboard that contains the scrolls of the Torah in a synagogue.

The Ark of the Covenant: now lost, the Ark contained the original Ten Commandments engraved in stone that Moses brought down from Mount Sinai.

Canaan: A land in ancient times which included most of modern Israel, Jordan, and Syria. It was considered by the ancient Israelites to be land promised to them by God. Also known as the Promised Land.

Circumcision: The removal of the foreskin from the penis, which is ritualistically done to Jewish boys eight days after birth. Circumcision marks the boy's entry into the covenant between God and the Jewish people.

Diaspora: The settling of scattered colonies of Jews outside Palestine after the Babylonian exile.

Exodus: The departure of the Israelites from slavery in Egypt in ancient times. Also, the name of the book in the Bible which tells this story.

Hebrew: A language spoken and written in ancient Palestine for more than a thousand years. Now the official language of the State of Israel.

Israel: The name of the state founded in 1948 in Palestine, intended to be the Jewish homeland. The term literally means "one who strives with God."

Jew: A person whose religious faith is Judaism, and who is descended from the ancient Jewish people.

Judah: A kingdom established in the south of Israel, when the kingdom of Israel split into two parts after the death of King Solomon in 928 BCE.

Judaism: The religion of the Jews, characterized by belief in one God and adherence to the Hebrew Scriptures.

Kabbalah: A collection of Jewish mystical knowledge, which explains how God created the universe, the ways he reveals himself, and his relationship with human beings. The Zohar, or Book of Splendor, is the most influential Kabbalistic text.

Kibbutz: An Israeli community where volunteers live and work collectively.

Kosher: Clean and prepared for use according to Jewish law. The term is usually applied to foods.

Menorah: A seven-branched candlestick, an ancient symbol of Judaism deriving from the menorah that originally stood in the Temple of Jerusalem.

Mezuzah: A parchment scroll with the first two paragraphs of the Shema handwritten on it, declaring the oneness of God and the special relationship between God and the Jewish people.

Midrash: A collection of sacred Jewish writings that gives in-depth explanations about the Talmud.

Mishnah: Sacred Judaic writings about the halakhot, or Jewish laws. The Mishnah together with the rabbis comments on it form the Talmud.

Orthodox Judaism: The branch of Jewish faith marked by strict adherence to traditional practice.

Palestine: The region of land where the Jews lived in ancient times.

Pogrom: An organized massacre of innocent people, often with the help of officials.

Prophet: A person who communicates with God in a special way and can act or speak on his behalf.

Psalms: A collection of praises to God.

Rabbi: A teacher who studies the Torah and applies it to daily life. A rabbi can lead services in synagogues and conduct weddings and funerals.

Sabbath/Shabbat: The day of rest and solemn assembly observed by Jews as sacred to God each week, from sunset Friday until sunset on Saturday.

Semitic: An adjective used to describe a group of people who lived in the land of Canaan in ancient times, from whom modern Jews descended.

Shofar: A ram's horn blown as a trumpet in synagogue during Rosh Hashanah and at Yom Kippur.

Star of David: A symbol of Judaism which signifies the protection of God given to David, King of Israel, around 970 BCE.

Stela: A pillar of stone that is inscribed for commemorative purposes.

Synagogue: The building or place of assembly used by Jews for religious worship. The word synagogue can also refer to an assembly of Jews gathered together to worship.

Talmud: The whole body of holy teachings in Judaism that explains the Bible and guides Jews in their daily lives. These teachings are also known as the oral Torah.

Temple of Jerusalem: The dwelling place for God constructed by King Solomon (970–928 BCE.) in Jerusalem in the era of the Israelite Empire. This First Temple was destroyed, then succeeded by the Second Temple, and then by the Third Temple. Of these, only the Wailing Wall remains today.

Torah: The Hebrew Bible, consisting of the first five books of the Christian Bible, plus Nevi'im (Prophets) and Ketuvim (holy writings). It includes the history of the Jews and their moral and legal code. The word "Torah" can also include the whole body of holy teachings that explains the Bible and guides Jews in their daily lives.

Wailing Wall: The most holy site in Judaism, the Wailing Wall is all that remains of the Second Temple of Jerusalem, which was destroyed by the Romans in 70 BCE.

Ziggurat: An ancient Babylonian temple that is built as a tall pyramidal structure surrounded by staircases, with a shrine at the top.

Zionist: A person who is committed to the Zionist movement's aim to establish and maintain a Jewish homeland in Palestine. The term Zionist is also used as an adjective to describe this movement.

INDEX

Acknowledgements

The Publishers would like to thank the following photographers and picture libraries for the photos used in this book.

t=top; tl=top left; tc=top center; tr=top right; c=center;
cl=center left; b=bottom; bl=bottom left; bc=bottom center; br=bottom right

Cover Corbis/Grazia Neri; **8bc** Corbis/Grazia Neri; **9t** Press Photo, Florence; **33cr** Corbis/Grazia Neri; **34c** Jersey Homesteads, Roosevelt New Jersey/Scala Group; **37c** Roger Ressmeyer/Starlight/Grazia Neri; **37br** Marco Ravenna/Fototeca Musei di Palazzo Pio; **41tl** Press Photo, Firenze